PIANO · VOCAL · GUITAR

CHART HITS OF
2014·2015

ISBN 978-1-4950-1229-7

HAL•LEONARD®
CORPORATION
7777 W. BLUEMOUND RD. P.O. BOX 13819 MILWAUKEE, WI 53213

Visit Hal Leonard Online at
www.halleonard.com

ALL ABOUT THAT BASS

Words and Music by KEVIN KADISH
and MEGHAN TRAINOR

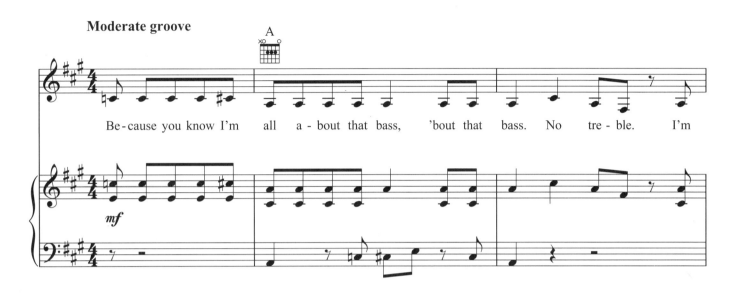

bass. No tre - ble. I'm all a - bout that bass, 'bout that bass. Be-cause you know I'm

bass.

ANIMALS

Words and Music by ADAM LEVINE,
BEN LEVIN and SHELLBACK

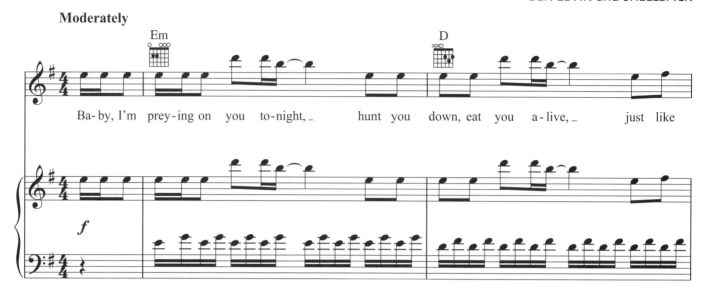

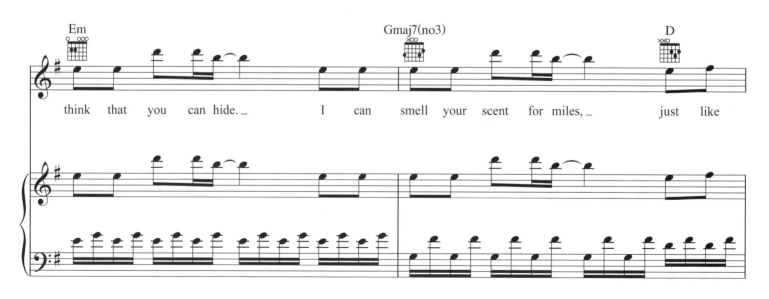

BANG BANG

Words and Music by ONIKA MARAJ,
MAX MARTIN, SAVAN KOTECHA
and RICKARD GÖRANSSON

With a groove

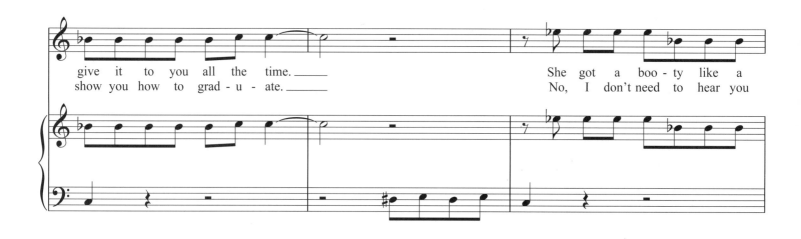

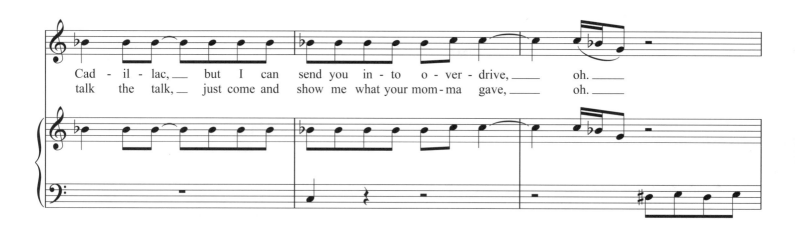

BLAME

Words and Music by CALVIN HARRIS, JOHN NEWMAN and JAMES NEWMAN

So blame it on the night, _____ don't blame it on ___ me, ___

don't blame it on ___ me, _____ don't blame it on ___ me. _____

COOL KIDS

Words and Music by GRAHAM SIEROTA,
JAMIE SIEROTA, NOAH SIEROTA,
SYDNEY SIEROTA, JEFFREY DAVID SIEROTA
and JESIAH DZWONEK

DON'T

Words and Music by ED SHEERAN,
DAWN ROBINSON, BEN LEVIN,
RAPHAEL SAADIQ, ALI JONES-MUHAMMAD
and CONESHA OWENS

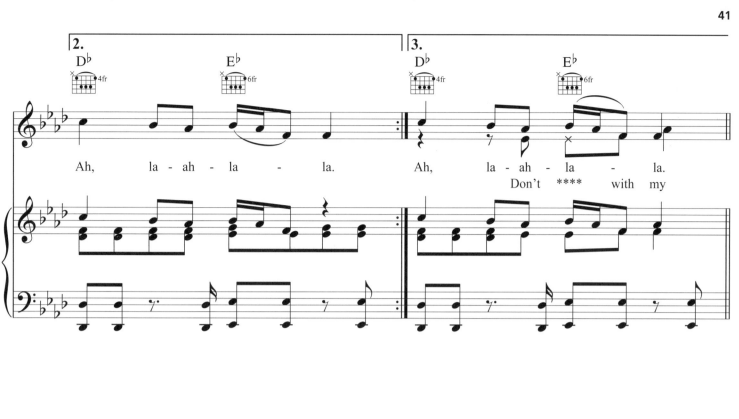

2.

Dᵇ   Eᵇ   **3.** Dᵇ   Eᵇ

Ah, la - ah - la - la.   Ah, la - ah - la - la.

Don't **** with my

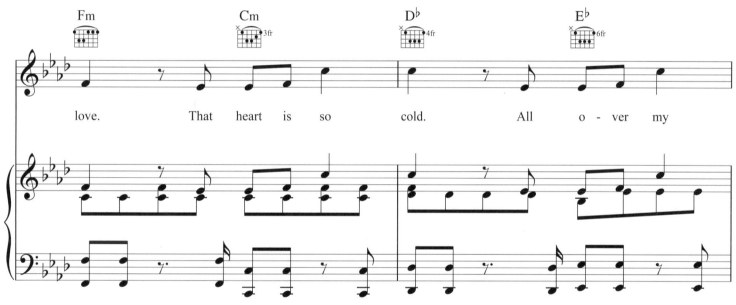

Fm   Cm   Dᵇ   Eᵇ

love.   That heart is so cold.   All o - ver my

Fm   Cm   Dᵇ   Eᵇ

home.___ I don't wan-na know that___ babe.   Ah, la - ah - la - la.

Don't **** with my

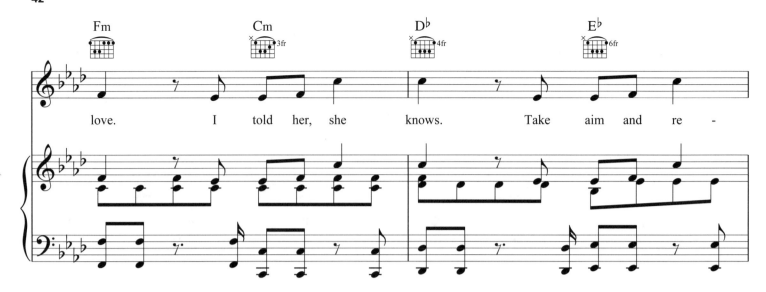

love.   I told her, she knows.   Take aim and re -

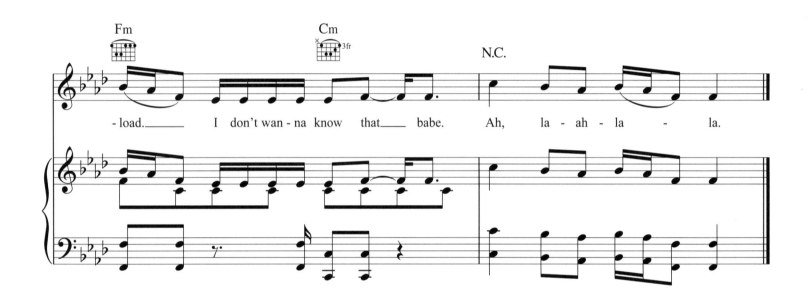

- load.____ I don't wan - na know that____ babe. Ah, la - ah - la - la.

Verse 3:

[Knock, knock, knock] on my hotel door.
I don't even know if she knows what for.
She was crying on my shoulder.
I already told ya.
Trust and respect is what we do this for.
I never intended to be next.
But you didn't need to take him to bed, that's all.
And I never saw him as a threat.
Until you disappeared with him to have sex, of course.
It's not like we were both on tour.
We were staying on the same ****ing hotel floor.
And I wasn't looking for a promise to commitment.
But it was never just fun and I thought you were different.
This is not the way you realise what you wanted.
It's a bit too much too late if I'm honest.
All this time, god knows, I'm singin':

HABITS
(Stay High)

Words and Music by TOVE LO,
JAKOB JERLSTRÖM and LUDVIG SÖDERBERG

Moderate Pop beat

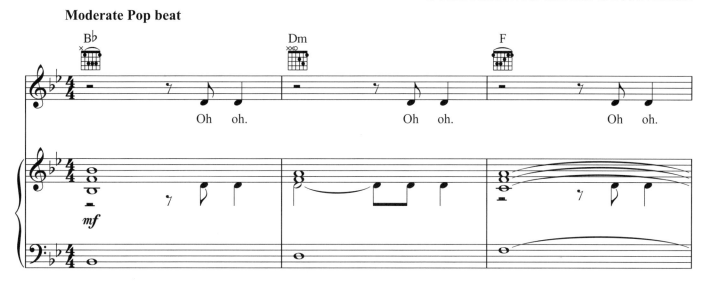

Oh oh.   Oh oh.   Oh oh.

I eat my din-ner in my bath-tub, then I go to

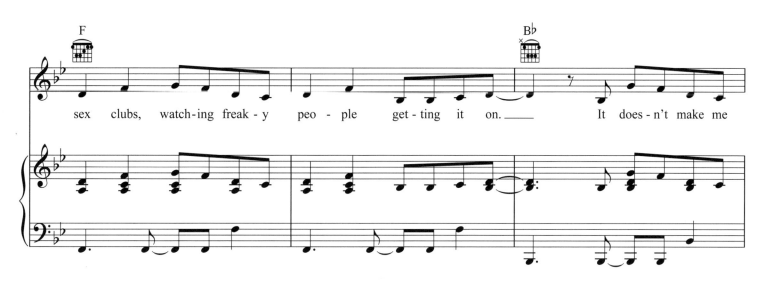

sex clubs, watch-ing freak-y peo-ple get-ting it on. _____ It does-n't make me

I'M NOT THE ONLY ONE

Words and Music by SAM SMITH
and JAMES NAPIER

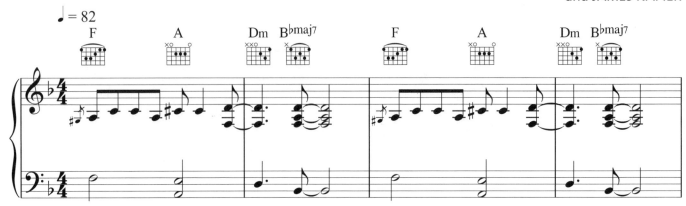

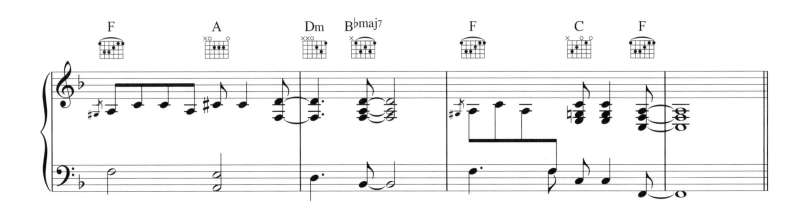

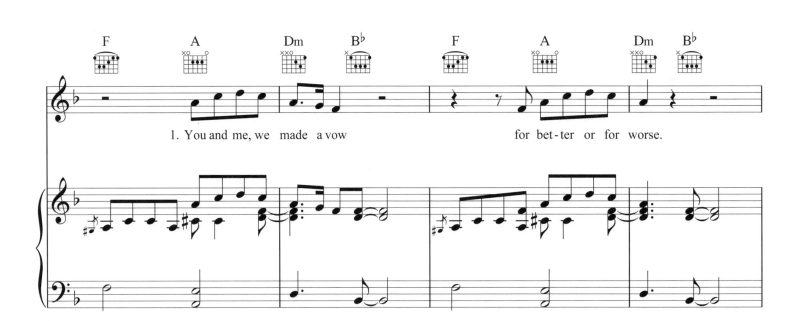

1. You and me, we made a vow   for bet-ter or for worse.

52

RIPTIDE

Words and Music by
VANCE JOY

Recorded a half step higher.

RUDE

Words and Music by NASRI ATWEH,
MARK PELLIZZER, ALEX TANAS,
BEN SPIVAK and ADAM MESSINGER

* Recorded a half step higher.

rude? _____

Can I have your daugh-ter for the rest of my life? __ Say yes, say yes, 'cause I

SHAKE IT OFF

Words and Music by TAYLOR SWIFT,
MAX MARTIN and SHELLBACK

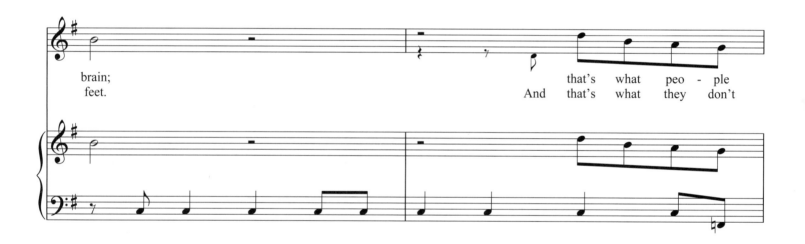

Additional Lyrics

Spoken: *Hey, hey, hey! Just think: While you've been getting*
Down and out about the liars and the dirty, dirty
Cheats of the world, you could've been getting down to
This. Sick. Beat!

Rap: My ex-man brought his new girlfriend.
She's like, "Oh, my god!" But I'm just gonna shake.
And to the fella over there with the hella good hair,
Won't you come on over, baby? We can shake, shake, shake.

A SKY FULL OF STARS

Words and Music by GUY BERRYMAN,
JON BUCKLAND, WILL CHAMPION,
CHRIS MARTIN and TIM BERGLING

*Recorded a half step higher.

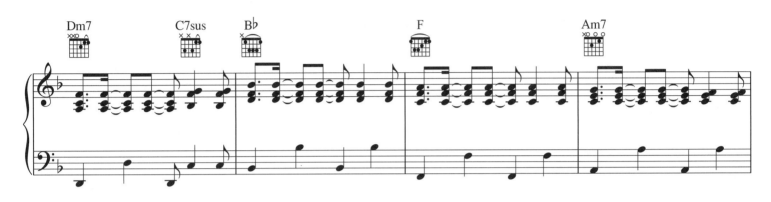

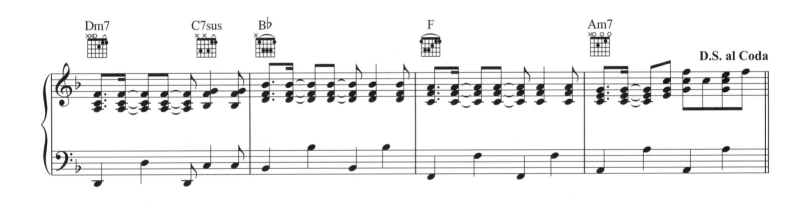

I think I see you.

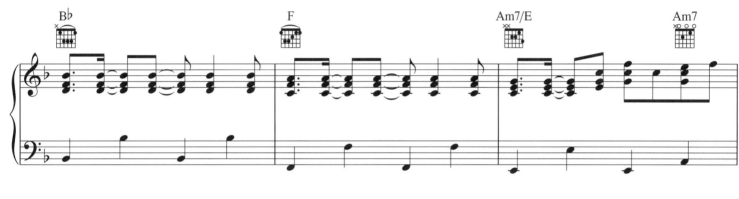

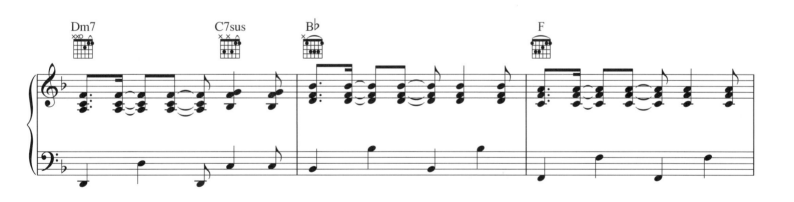

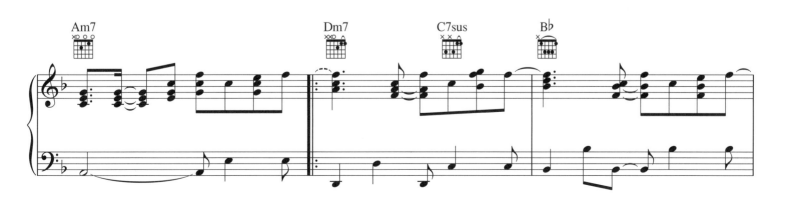

'Cause you're a sky, ___ you're a sky ___ full of stars, ___

___ such a heav - en - ly view. ___

You're such a heav-en-ly view.

STEAL MY GIRL

Words and Music by LOUIS TOMLINSON,
LIAM PAYNE, JULIAN BUNETTA,
WAYNE HECTOR, EDWARD DREWETT
and JOHN RYAN

Moderate Rock beat

SUPERHEROES

Words and Music by DANIEL O'DONOGHUE,
MARK SHEEHAN and JAMES BARRY

Moderately slow

All her life,___ she has seen___ all the mean-

-er side ___ of mean.___ They took a-way___ the proph-et's dream___ for a prof-

YELLOW FLICKER BEAT

from THE HUNGER GAMES: MOCKINGJAY PART 1

Words and Music by ELLA YELICH O'CONNOR
and JOEL LITTLE

Moderate Electro Pop

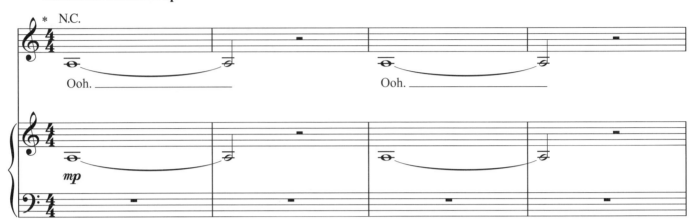

Ooh. _____ Ooh. _____

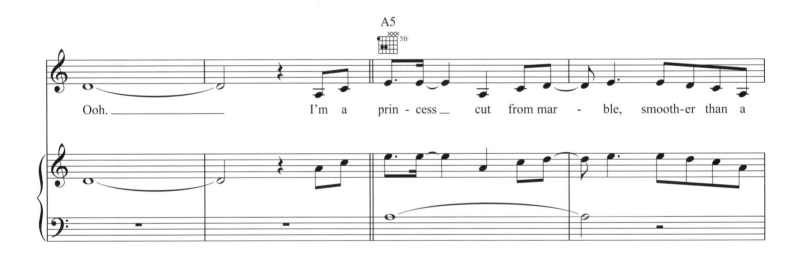

Ooh. _____ I'm a prin-cess _ cut from mar - ble, smooth-er than a

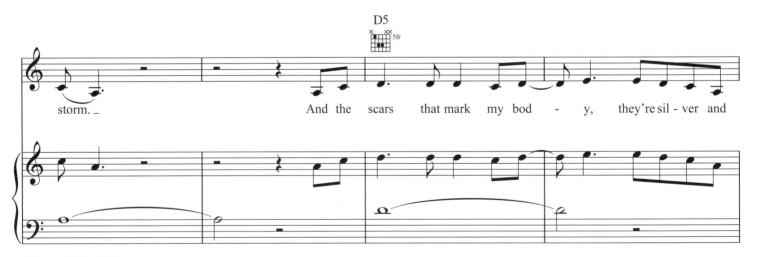

storm. _ And the scars that mark my bod - y, they're sil - ver and

* *Recorded a half step lower.*

TAKE ME TO CHURCH

Words and Music by
ANDREW HOZIER-BYRNE

Moderate Ballad

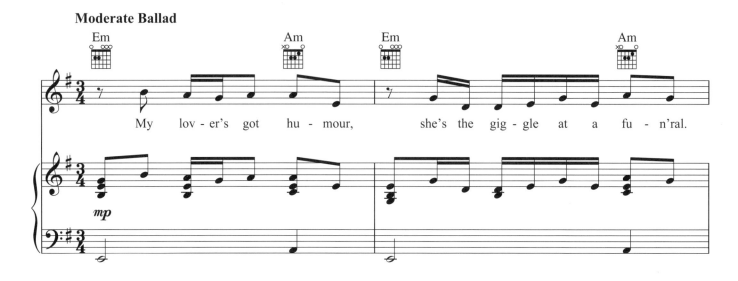

My lov-er's got hu-mour, she's the gig-gle at a fu-n'ral.

Knows ev-'ry-bod-y's dis-ap-prov-al, I should've wor-shipped her soon-er.

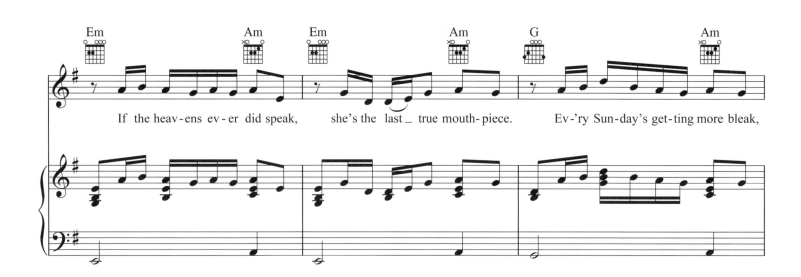

If the heav-ens ev-er did speak, she's the last __ true mouth-piece. Ev-'ry Sun-day's get-ting more bleak,

100